Grammar One

Jennifer Seidl

Oxford University Press

Contents

1 Hello! I'm Jenny

Hello! My name**'s** Jenny Bell. And this **is** Nick. **He's** my brother. **He's** twelve.

Jenny**'s** my sister. **She's** nine.

I'm not. **I'm** eleven!

We're from Merton, near London.

And this **is** Chip. **He's** a good dog.

And what**'s** your name? Where **are you** from?

I am . . . **I'm** . . . er . . . **Am I** . . . ?

This **is** Trig, a very special friend. **He isn't** from Merton. **He's** from planet Triglon.

Grammar lesson

Subject pronouns

Singular	**I**
	you
	he
	she
	it
Plural	**we**
	you
	they

he, she or **it**?

A person is **he**   or **she**.

A thing is **it**.

An animal is **it**   or **he/she** (for example, a pet).

▶ *Jenny* / *She* } **is eleven**.   *Nick* / *He* } **is twelve**.

Jenny and Nick / *They* } **are from Merton**.

Present simple of be

	Long forms		Short forms		Questions
Singular	I am	I am not	I'm	I'm not	am I?
	you are	you are not	you're	you aren't	are you?
	he is	he is not	he's	he isn't	is he?
	she is	she is not	she's	she isn't	is she?
	it is	it is not	it's	it isn't	is it?
Plural	we are	we are not	we're	we aren't	are we?
	you are	you are not	you're	you aren't	are you?
	they are	they are not	they're	they aren't	are they?

Also: What **is**/What's . . . ? My name **is**/My name's . . .

Short answers
Are you from Merton? **Yes, I am.** OR **No, I'm not.**
Is Nick twelve? **Yes, he is.**
Is Jenny twelve? **No, she isn't.**

1 What's missing?

Write in the missing words.

Long forms	Short forms
we are	▶ we're
he is	1
2	I'm
3	she isn't
you are not	4
we are not	5
6	they're
7	it's
I am not	8
he is not	9

2 Hello!

a Write **am**, **is** or **are**.

Hello! I ▶ *am* Nick and

this __1__ Jenny.

She __2__ my sister.

We __3__ brother and sister.

I __4__ twelve and Jenny

__5__ eleven.

We __6__ from Merton.

Merton __7__ near London.

What __8__ your name?

Where __9__ you from?

This __10__ our friend Trig.

He __11__ a visitor from planet Triglon.

b Now say the sentences.

3 What's your name?

a Write the short forms.

Hello! What ►'s _____ your name?

I ¹_____ Jenny, and this is Nick.

He ²_____ my brother.

We ³_____ brother and sister.

He ⁴_____ twelve and I ⁵_____

eleven. We ⁶_____ from Merton.

This is Trig. He ⁷_____ our friend.

He ⁸_____ from Merton.

He ⁹_____ from Triglon.

And this is Chip. He ¹⁰_____ our dog.

b Now say the sentences.

4 Change the sentences

Say **he**, **she**, **it** or **they**.

► Jenny is eleven.
   She is eleven.
► Trig isn't from Merton.
   He isn't from Merton.

1 Nick isn't eleven.
2 Merton is near London.
3 Nick is twelve.
4 Jenny isn't twelve.
5 Nick and Jenny are brother and sister.
6 Trig is a good friend.
7 Mr and Mrs Bell are from Merton.
8 Merton is a small town.
9 Trig is a visitor from Triglon.
10 Triglon is a small planet.
11 Chip is a good dog.
12 Chip is four years old.

5 Arrange the words

Write ten true sentences. Use the words in three blocks for each sentence, in the order 1, 2, 3.

► Jenny is from Merton.
► She is from Merton.

_____

_____

_____

_____

_____

_____

_____

_____

| ³ eleven. | ¹ They | ¹ She | ¹ Nick |

| ² is | ¹ Jenny | ³ from Triglon. |

| ³ from Merton. | ¹ Trig | ³ twelve. |

| ¹ Nick and Jenny | ² are | ¹ He |

6 Friends

Jenny is in the bus with Zoe and Carlo.
Zoe is from Greece. She's thirteen.
Carlo is from Italy. He's twelve.

Nick is in the park with Maria and George.
Maria is from Italy. She's thirteen.
George is from Greece. He's eleven.

a Where are they from? How old are they?
Say what is the same.

▶ Maria and Carlo
  Maria and Carlo are from Italy.

1 George and Zoe
2 Zoe and Maria
3 Nick and Jenny
4 Nick and Carlo
5 Jenny and George

b Give a short answer.

▶ Is Nick from England?
  Yes, he is.

▶ Are Zoe and Carlo in the park?
  No, they aren't.

1 Is Nick in the park?
2 Is Nick with Zoe and Carlo?
3 Are Maria and George in the bus?
4 Is Jenny in the bus?
5 Are Maria, George and Nick
  in the park?
6 Are Zoe and Carlo with Jenny?
7 Is Carlo twelve?
8 Are Zoe and Maria thirteen?
9 Is Zoe from Greece?
10 Is Carlo from Greece?
11 Is Jenny thirteen?
12 Is George eleven?
13 Are Nick and Carlo twelve?
14 Is Maria from Italy?
15 Is Maria from England?
16 Are Nick and Zoe from Italy?
17 Is Carlo eleven?
18 Are you from England?
19 Are you from Greece?
20 Are you eleven?

2 A big book for Trig Articles; Adjectives

Look, Trig!
Here's **a big** book for you.
It's very **thick**.

And here's **a little** book.
It's very **thin**.

The big book's **an English** dictionary.
A dictionary is a **useful** book.

The little book is a grammar.
A grammar's **an important** book, too.

Yes, **a** dictionary's
a very **useful** book!

Grammar lesson

Articles: **a/an, the**

a /ə/	before a consonant sound:
	▶ *a book, a thick book*
	▶ *a yellow book, a useful book*

an /ən/	before a vowel sound:
	▶ *an important book*

the /ðə/	before a consonant sound:
	▶ *the book, the yellow book*

the /ðɪ/	before a vowel sound:
	▶ *the English book*

Position of adjectives

We put adjectives

1 before a noun:
   ▶ *a big book, a good dog*

2 after a verb:
   ▶ *The book is thick.   Chip is good.*

Nationality adjectives

Country	Adjective/Language
America	**American**
Egypt	**Egyptian**
England	**English**
France	**French**
Germany	**German**
Greece	**Greek**
Italy	**Italian**
Spain	**Spanish**
Turkey	**Turkish**

▶ *an English boy*   *Dimitris is Greek.*
  the Turkish language   *Carlo is Italian.*

Write the country, the language and the adjective with a capital letter.

1 What's in the picnic basket?

Write a list with **a** or **an**.

a	an
a banana	an egg

2 Guess the words

Write the words correctly.

► an *ye   an eye

► a *rothe* a brother

1 an *rm

2 a *ister

3 a *esson

4 a *choo*

5 an *mbrell*

6 a *ather

7 an *range

8 an *pp*e

9 an *gg

10 a **cycl*

11 a *aske*

12 a *ootba**

13 an *nimal

14 a *ook

15 an *xerc*se

16 a *ette*

3 Memory game

Look at the picture for one minute.
Close the book.

a Name the twelve things on the table,
using **a** or **an**.

b Now name the twelve things on the table,
using **the**.

4 Get it right

Put the words in order and make sentences.

▶ | dog. | Chip | a | is | | Chip | is | a | good | dog. |

▶ *Chip is a good dog.*

1 | Trig | a | friend. | special | is | _____

2 | not | is | Triglon | a | planet. | big | _____

3 | town. | a | Merton | is | small | _____

4 | is | big. | not | grammar book | The | _____

5 | The | very | is | dictionary | thick. | _____

6 | are | Jenny | English. | and | Nick | _____

7 | Italian. | Carlo | and | are | Maria | _____

8 | Greek | is | a | Dimitris | name. | _____

9 | Carlo | an | name. | Italian | is | _____

10 | not | is | English | Trig | name. | an | _____

5 What are they?

Put in **a** or **an** and a nationality adjective. Use:

American   Greek
Egyptian   Italian
English   Spanish
French   Turkish
German

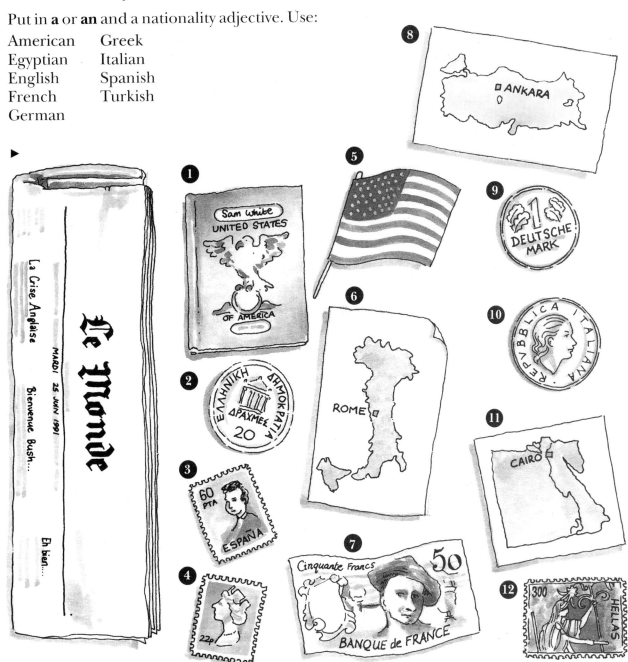

▶ It's _a French_ _____ newspaper.

1 It's _____ passport.

2 It's _____ coin.

3 It's _____ stamp.

4 It's _____ stamp.

5 It's _____ flag.

6 It's _____ city.

7 It's _____ banknote.

8 It's _____ city.

9 It's _____ coin.

10 It's _____ coin

11 It's _____ city.

12 It's _____ stamp.

3 Girls and boys   Plural of nouns

Who's in the road?

I can see a man, a woman with a baby, and two old **ladies** on a bench.

At the bus stop I can see two **men** and two **women**. Also three **children** – a boy and two **girls**. The boy is Nick and one of the **girls** is Jenny.

And look – it's Trig in the **bushes**!

Grammar lesson

Plural of nouns

Regular plurals

	Singular	Plural
Add **s**	girl	girl**s**
	boy	boy**s**
Add **es** to **ch**	bench	bench**es**
o	tomato	tomato**es**
s	bus	bus**es**
sh	bush	bush**es**
x	box	box**es**
y after consonant → **ies**	baby	bab**ies**
	lady	lad**ies**

Irregular plurals

Singular	Plural
child	child**ren**
man	men
woman	women
person	**people**
tooth	teeth
foot	feet

Pronunciation

/s/ after /p, t, k, ʃ, θ/: *shops, books*
/ɪz/ after /s, z, ʃ, ʒ, tʃ, dʒ/: *buses, benches*
/z/ after other sounds: *girls, tomatoes*

1   Making lists

a   Write the plurals in the correct lists.

cup ✓	friend	car	dictionary
class ✓	bus	desk	child
road	country	woman	glass
box	bush	watch	potato
foot	shirt	girl	person
tomato	city	tree	day
beach	bench	party	policeman
story	boy	match	dog
pen	baby	dish	

s	es	ies
▶ *cups*	▶ *classes*	_____
_____	_____	_____
_____	_____	_____
_____	_____	_____
_____	_____	_____
_____	_____	**Irregular**
_____	_____	_____
_____	_____	_____
_____	_____	_____
_____	_____	_____

b   Now read out your lists.

2 At the market

Complete the labels. Now say the words.

▶ GRAPE **S**____   BANANA _____

POTATO _____   FIG _____

RADISH _____   DATE _____

STRAWBERR _____   MELON _____

LEMON _____   CHERR _____

ORANGE _____   PEACH _____   TOMATO _____

3 Word square

Ring the plural words.
Are there 12, 16 or 20?

```
W  O  M  E  N  P  B  G  C  A  R  S  L
B  O  Y  S  D  E  X  L  A  R  M  X  A
D  I  C  T  I  O  N  A  R  I  E  S  D
S  H  I  P  S  P  X  S  X  Y  N  I  I
R  L  T  E  H  L  J  S  H  O  E  S  E
S  X  I  N  E  E  X  E  G  G  S  X  S
Y  P  E  A  S  Q  Q  S  B  O  X  E  S
B  U  S  E  S  X  C  L  A  S  S  E  S
A  S  C  H  I  L  D  R  E  N  Y  A  Q
F  E  E  T  X  N  X  T  E  E  T  H  Y
```

4 In the park

Spot the differences. Write what you can see.

In **Picture A** I can see . . .

▶ *one woman*

1 _____   6 _____
2 _____   7 _____
3 _____   8 _____
4 _____   9 _____
5 _____   10 _____

In **Picture B** I can see . . .

▶ *two women*

11 _____   16 _____
12 _____   17 _____
13 _____   18 _____
14 _____   19 _____
15 _____   20 _____

4 Meet my teacher   Possessive adjectives

Meet **my** teacher.
She's small and fair.
Her name is Miss Mill.

Now meet **my** teacher.
He's tall and dark.
His name is Mr Blake.

Here's **our** school.
It's in Park Street.
Its name is Park Street School.

PARK
STREET
SCHOOL

Here are **our** friends.
Their names are Amanda and Tom.

Grammar lesson

Pronouns	Possessive adjectives
I	**my**
you	**your**
he	**his**
she	**her**
it	**its**
we	**our**
you	**your**
they	**their**

▶ *I am a good friend.* **My** *name is Trig.*
We are from Merton. **Our** *surname is Bell.*

1   Her name is . . .

Put in **your**, **his**, **her**, **its** or **their**.

Jenny and Nick are from Merton. ▶ *Their*
surname is Bell. 1_____ friends, Tom
and Amanda, are from Merton too. Jenny's
eleven. 2_____ eyes are blue. 3_____
hair is yellow. 4_____ brother Nick is
twelve. 5_____ eyes and hair are brown.
6_____ dog is Chip. 7_____ eyes are
brown and 8_____ hair is black and white.

9_____ school is in Park Street. It's near
10_____ house. 11_____ name is Park
Street School. Jenny's teacher is very
friendly. 12_____ name is Miss Mill.
Nick's teacher is nice, too. 13_____ name
is Mr Blake.

What about you? What's 14_____ name?
Where's 15_____ school? What's
16_____ name? And 17_____ friends?
What are 18_____ names?

2 Favourites

	Jenny	Nick	Mr and Mrs Bell	You
Music	rock	rock	opera	?
Singer	Prince	Sting	Pavarotti	?
Sport	swimming	football	tennis	?
Food	chocolate cake	ice-creams	pizza	?

Talk about Jenny, Nick, Mr and Mrs Bell and you.
Use **her**, **his**, **their** and **my**.

▶ *Her favourite music is rock.* ▶ *Her favourite singer is Prince.*

3 Guessing game

Look at the pictures. Look at their hair.
Look at their favourite sport, food and colour.
Now choose a boy or girl.
Ask the class to guess who it is.

▶ YOU *It's a girl.*
    CLASS *Is her hair dark?*
    YOU *Yes, it is.*
    CLASS *Is her hair long?*
    YOU *No, it isn't.*
    CLASS *Is her favourite colour red?*
    YOU *No, it isn't.*
    CLASS *Is it Kate?*
    YOU *Yes, it is!*

Mary   **Ann**   **Liz**
swimming   tennis   swimming
pizza   chicken   pizza
blue   blue   red

Kate   **Jane**   **Rob**   **Alex**   **Paul**   **Ben**   **Mike**
tennis   swimming   football   basketball football   football   basketball
spaghetti chicken   steak   spaghetti   spaghetti steak   beefburgers
pink   pink   green   red   orange   blue   orange

4 Ask your partner

Choose a partner. Ask and answer ten questions about
favourites, like this:

▶ YOU *What is your favourite colour?*
    PARTNER *My favourite colour is orange.*

Talk about colours, lessons, animals, food, drink,
singers, songs, TV programmes, hobbies, sports, games.

5 Is it Nick's? Possessives

Is it Jenny**'s** skateboard or Nick**'s**?

Are they the girl**s'** bicycles or the boy**s'**?

Is it the children**'s** ball or the dog**'s**?

And whose exercise book is this . . . ?

Grammar lesson

Possessives

1 Use **'s** or **s'** with people and animals.

Singular	It's Nick**'s** skateboard.
	OR It's Nick**'s**.
	It's the dog**'s** ball.
	OR It's the dog**'s**.
	They're Jenny**'s** cassettes.
	OR They're Jenny**'s**.
Plural	They're the girl**s'** bicycles.
	OR They're the girl**s'**.
	They're the boy**s'** skateboards.
	OR They're the boy**s'**.

2 Use **'s** with irregular plurals.
▶ *I'm the children**'s** friend.*

Possessive	*Short form of* **is**
the dog**'s** ball =	Chip**'s** the dog. =
the ball of the dog	Chip is the dog.

1 Nick talks about his pictures

Ring the possessives and the short forms.
Then write two lists.

Look, this is my best friend. His name's Tom
Allen. This is the Allens' house. Look at
Tom's old bicycle. And look at Mr Allen's old
car. The Walkman's Tom's.

And this is Jenny's best friend. Her name's
Amanda Todd. Amanda's twelve. This is the
Todds' house. Amanda's bicycle's new. This
is Chip's old ball. And this is the Todds' car.

Possessives	**Short forms**
▶ *Allens'*	▶ *name's*

2 Who are they?

Say and write sentences.

▶ Mrs Allen? (mother)
Mrs Allen is Tom's mother.

1 Mrs Todd? (mother)

_____

2 Mr Allen? (father)

_____

3 Mr Blake? (teacher)

_____

4 Amanda? (daughter)

_____

5 Jenny? (sister)

_____

6 Mr Todd? (father)

_____

7 Chip? (dog)

_____

8 Trig? (friend)

_____

9 Amanda? (best friend)

_____

10 Miss Mill? (teacher)

_____

11 Tom? (best friend)

_____

12 Jenny and Nick? (children)

_____

3 Names

Name the people you know.
Then write sentences.

▶ sister/sisters
My sister's name is Anna. OR
My sisters' names are Anna and Susan.

1 English teacher

_____

2 brother/brothers

_____

3 best friend/friends

_____

4 father

_____

5 mother

_____

6 uncle/uncles

_____

7 aunt/aunts

_____

8 cousin/cousins

_____

9 doctor

_____

10 pen-friend

_____

11 pet/pets

_____

12 neighbour/neighbours

_____

6 What have the Bells got?

Look! The Bells **have got** a new car.
It has got four doors, and **it's got** a radio.
Has it **got** a sunroof? No, it **hasn't**.

Grammar lesson

Present simple of **have got**

Use **have got** for possession.

Long forms		*Short forms*	
I **have**		I**'ve**	
you **have**		you**'ve**	
he **has**		he**'s**	
she **has**	**got**	she**'s**	**got**
it **has**		it**'s**	
we **have**		we**'ve**	
you **have**		you**'ve**	
they **have**		they**'ve**	

I **have not got**	I **haven't got**
he **has not got**	he **hasn't got**

Questions
Have I **got**?
Has he **got**?

Short answers
Have you got a new car?
Yes, I have. OR **No, I haven't.**
Has your friend got a new car?
Yes, she has. OR **No, she hasn't.**

No **got** in short answers!

Present simple of **have got**

1 What have you got?

Look at the pictures. Say what you/your
family **have got** and what you **haven't got**.
Make fourteen sentences.

► *I've got a watch, but I haven't got a doll.*
► *We've got a cat, but we haven't got a dog.*

2 What's in the school bags?

a Say what the children have got and what they haven't got.

▶ Jenny
*Jenny has got an atlas, a paint box, a brush and a pencil.
She hasn't got an exercise book.*

1 Tom

4 Amanda

2 Nick

5 Maria

3 Carlo

6 Zoe

Have two children got the same things?

b Ask five pupils what they have got in their school bags. Make questions like this:

▶ YOU   *Have you got a pencil?*
PUPIL   *Yes, I have.* OR *No, I haven't.*

3 Partner game

a Write six sentences with **I've got** . . .

Use:

Colours	Things
red	sweater
blue	T-shirt
green	pen
yellow	exercise book
white	school bag
black	bicycle

▶ *I've got a green sweater.*
▶ *I've got a red T-shirt.*

_____

_____

_____

_____

_____

_____

b Now guess the things on your partner's list.

▶ YOU   *Have you got a white sweater?*
PARTNER *No, I haven't.*
YOU   *Have you got a green sweater?*
PARTNER *Yes, I have.*

4 Look at Trig!

Look at this picture of Trig. Use the words in the list to ask questions about him.

▶ YOU   *Has he got a fat body?*
CLASS *Yes, he has.*

big	body
small	ears
long	face
fat	socks
funny	hat
striped	shirt
	scarf

7 These are mine Demonstratives; Possessive pronouns

Grammar lesson

Demonstratives

Singular	**this**	OR	**this** cassette
	that	OR	**that** cassette
Plural	**these**	OR	**these** cassettes
	those	OR	**those** cassettes

this ice-cream   **these** ice-creams

that   **those**

Possessive pronouns

Adjectives	*Pronouns*
my	**mine**
your	**yours**
his	**his**
her	**hers**
our	**ours**
your	**yours**
their	**theirs**

▶ *It's my book.* OR *It's **mine**.*
They're her books. OR *They're **hers**.*

*These are **ours** and those are **yours**.*
*Is that the Bells' car? Yes, it's **theirs**.*

1 These and those

Make correct sentences.

▶   This is/These are   my orange juice.
      This is my orange juice.

1	These are/Those are	our beefburgers over there.
2	This is/These are	Jenny's cheeseburger.
3	That's/This is	your Coke here.
4	This is/These are	Tom's ice-creams.
5	That's/Those are	Amanda's chocolate cake.
6	This is/That's	Chip's bone in the garden.
7	These are/Those are	her crisps over there.
8	Those are/That's	Nick's lemonade.
9	These are/This is	Jenny's ice-lolly.
10	And those are/these are	Trig's three giant milk-shakes over there!

2 This exercise . . .

Put in **this is** or **these are**.

▶ Look, *this is* _____ Nick's jacket  and *these are* _____ his shoes.

1 _____ Jenny's gloves and _____ her school bag.

2 _____ Nick's cap and _____ his socks.

3 _____ Mr Bell's watch and _____ his umbrella.

4 _____ the children's books and _____ their snacks.

5 _____ Trig's scarf and _____ his boots.

---

3 Missing words

Look at the table of possessive pronouns in the grammar lesson for one minute.
Cover the table. Put in the missing words.

I	▶ my	▶ mine
you	1	2
3	4	his
she	5	6
we	7	8
9	your	10
they	11	12

4 His, hers or theirs?

Look at Exercise 2 and answer the questions.

▶ Are the gloves Jenny's?
Yes, they're hers. _____

▶ Is the jacket Trig's?
No, it's not his. _____

1 Is the cap Nick's?

_____

2 Are the shoes Jenny's?

_____

3 Are the books the children's?

_____

4 Is the watch Nick's?

_____

5 Are the snacks the children's?

_____

6 Is the school bag Jenny's?

_____

7 Are the socks Trig's?

_____

8 A picnic   Countable and uncountable nouns

> I've got **a** banana, three apples, **an** orange and **some** biscuits.

> I've got **some** bread, **some** cheese and **some** milk.

> I've got **some** orange juice and **some** crisps.

1 A picnic

Write **a**, **an** or **some**.

▶ *a* _____ milk-shake
▶ *some* _____ sugar

1 _____ lemonade
2 _____ butter

3 _____ sandwich
4 _____ eggs
5 _____ jam

6 _____ chips
7 _____ apple
8 _____ chocolate
9 _____ biscuit
10 _____ sweets

11 _____ cherries
12 _____ ice-cream

2 Right or wrong?

Put a ✓ for Right and a ✗ for Wrong.

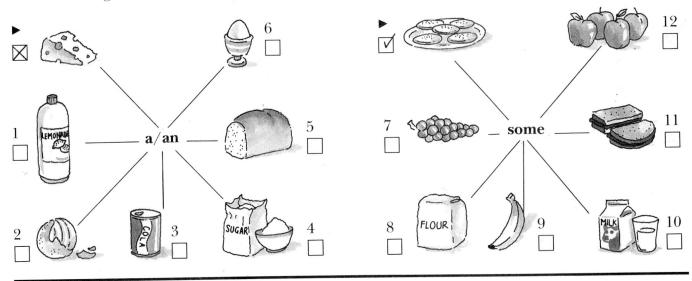

3 What have they got?

Use **a**, **an** or **some** to write what they've got.

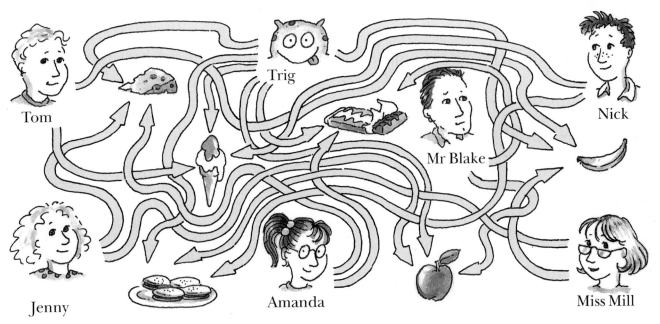

Jenny's got ▶ _some cheese_ and ▶ _an apple_ .

Nick's got [1]_____ and [2]_____ .

Amanda's got [3]_____ and [4]_____ .

Miss Mill's got [5]_____ and [6]_____ .

Tom's got [7]_____ and [8]_____ .

Mr Blake's got [9]_____ and [10]_____ .

Trig's got [11]_____ , [12]_____ , [13]_____

[14]_____ , [15]_____ and [16]_____ .

9 I like school   Present simple with **I**, **you**, **we** and **they**

On weekdays Jenny and Nick **get up** at seven thirty. They **walk** to school every day. They **wear** uniforms.

I **like** school. It's fun.

I **don't like** school. I **hate** Maths and English.

They **go** home at three thirty. Then they **do** their homework – well, not always.

After dinner they **watch** television. They **don't go** to bed until nine o'clock.

Grammar lesson

Present simple with **I**, **you**, **we** and **they**

I
you
we   } **like**
they

I
you
we   } **do not** OR
they   **don't like**

Use the present simple

1   for repeated actions, often with time phrases such as **on weekdays**, **every day/week/Saturday**:
    ▸ *On weekdays they **get up** at seven thirty.*
       *They **walk** to school every day.*

2   for facts which do not change:
    ▸ *The children **wear** uniforms.*

3   with verbs such as **love**, **hate**, **like**, **dislike**:
    ▸ *I **don't like** school. I **hate** Maths.*

1 Jenny and Nick's day

Put in **do** (x 2), **get up**, **go** (x 2), **have** (x 2), **play**, **start**, **walk**, **watch**.

Jenny and Nick ▸ *get up* at seven thirty.

They ___1___ breakfast at eight.

They ___2___ to school.

Lessons ___3___ at nine o'clock.

The children ___4___ lunch at school.

They ___5___ more work after lunch, or they ___6___ games.

They ___7___ home at three thirty.

Then they ___8___ their homework before dinner.

After dinner they ___9___ television, and they ___10___ to bed at nine o'clock.

2 Your day

Compare Jenny and Nick's day with your day. Say what you do.

▸   Jenny and Nick get up at seven thirty.
    I get up at seven o'clock. OR
    I get up at seven thirty, too.

1   Jenny and Nick have breakfast at eight o'clock.
2   They walk to school.
3   Their lessons start at nine o'clock.
4   They work from nine to one.
5   They have lunch at school.
6   They play games in the afternoon.
7   They go home at three thirty.
8   They do their homework before dinner.
9   After dinner they watch television.
10 They go to bed at nine o'clock.
11 They read comics in bed.
12 They go to sleep at nine thirty.

3 Nick's class

a Say what the pupils **like** and what they **don't like**.

	🙂	🙁
Maths	5	15
English	14	6
Geography	11	9
History	12	8
Science	10	10
Games	18	2
Music	13	7
Art	16	4

▶ *Five pupils like Maths and fifteen pupils don't like Maths.*

b Now say what you **like** and what you **don't like**.

▶ *I like English, but I don't like History.*

4 Hobbies and interests

Say what you do and what you don't do in your free time.

▶ read magazines
I read magazines.
▶ go fishing
I don't go fishing.

1 read books
2 watch television
3 read comics
4 listen to the radio
5 collect stamps
6 play the piano
7 play football
8 go swimming
9 read newspapers
10 collect posters
11 collect stickers
12 play the guitar
13 listen to music
14 play basketball
15 go riding
16 play tennis

5 Nature quiz

These sentences are wrong. Correct them like this:

▶ Birds fly under water. _Wrong._
Birds don't fly under water.
They fly in the air.

1 Pandas live in Africa. _____

2 Fish swim in the air. _____

3 Bananas grow in cold countries. _____

4 Kangaroos live in India. _____

5 Peanuts grow on trees. _____

6 Penguins live at the North Pole. _____

7 Koalas eat fish. _____

in the ground   leaves
in Australia   at the South Pole
under water   in the air ✓
in China   in hot countries

10 Chip likes ice-creams

Present simple with **he**, **she** and **it**

Chip **likes** ice-creams and smelly bones.
He **buries** his bones in the flower beds.
He **watches** cartoons on television.

Unfortunately, he **doesn't like** Fluff,
the neighbours' cat.

He **chases** her every day!

Grammar lesson

Present simple with **he**, **she** and **it**

he		he	
she	} **likes**	she	} **does not** OR
it		it	**doesn't like**

Remember the **s**   **like**s
after he/she/it!   **does**n't like

> ▶ Chip **likes** ice-creams and smelly bones.
>   He **doesn't like** the neighbours' cat.

Add **es** to *ch, o, s, sh* and *x*:

watch	he/she/it watch**es**
do	he/she/it do**es**
miss	he/she/it miss**es**
wash	he/she/it wash**es**
mix	he/she/it mix**es**

y after consonant → **ies**:

bury	he/she/it bur**ies**
carry	he/she/it carr**ies**
try	he/she/it tr**ies**

do → does /dʌz/
go → goes /gəʊz/
say → says /sez/

1 Make lists

These verbs have got different endings
with he/she/it. Write them in three lists.

play ✓	try	hurry	go	do
watch ✓	buy	learn	start	do
carry ✓	miss	say	dry	teach
see	walk	mix	come	fix
wash	bury	cry	fry	

s	es	ies
▶ *plays*	▶ *watches*	▶ *carries*

2 Daily timetable

Write your name and the times.

Name _____		
▶ I get up	at	*seven thirty*
I eat breakfast	at	_____
I go to school	at	_____
I leave school	at	_____
I eat lunch	at	_____
I do my homework	at	_____
I eat dinner	at	_____
I watch television	at	_____
I go to bed	at	_____
I fall asleep	at	_____

Exchange books with a partner. Read out to
the class what your partner does, like this:

> ▶ *He/She gets up at seven o'clock.*
> ▶ *He/She eats breakfast at seven thirty.*

3 Chip likes to help

Put in the verbs with the correct endings.

sleep	In summer Chip ▶ *sleeps* in the garden.
wake	He <u>1 </u> up very early.
bark, make	He <u>2 </u> at the birds and <u>3 </u> a lot of noise.
do	He <u>4 </u> n't like the postman. He sometimes
tear	<u>5 </u> his trousers.
dig	He <u>6 </u> holes in the flower beds and
bury	<u>7 </u> his smelly bones.
chase	Every day he <u>8 </u> Fluff, the neighbours' cat,
catch	but he never <u>9 </u> her.
go	He <u>10 </u> to the shops with Mrs Bell.
carry	He <u>11 </u> her shopping bag or newspapers in
like	his mouth. He <u>12 </u> shopping. Unfortunately
chew	he <u>13 </u> the newspapers, and when he
see, drop	<u>14 </u> a cat he <u>15 </u> the shopping bag
run, love	and <u>16 </u> off. He <u>17 </u> to help!

---

4 Food

Say what they like and what they don't like.

▶ *Jenny likes peaches, but she doesn't like plums.*
Nick likes plums, but he doesn't like peaches.
Trig likes peaches and plums.
Chip doesn't like peaches or plums.

	Jenny	Nick	Trig	Chip
peaches	✓	✗	✓	✗
plums	✗	✓	✓	✗
carrots	✓	✗	✓	✗
spinach	✗	✓	✓	✗
milk-shakes	✓	✗	✓	✗
fizzy drinks	✓	✓	✓	✗
eggs	✗	✗	✓	✗
pizza	✓	✗	✗	✗
steaks	✓	✓	✗	✓
smelly bones	✗	✗	✗	✓

5 Class game

Have you got a good memory?
Play this game round the class.
Say what you don't like.

▶ PUPIL A   *I don't like snakes.*
  PUPIL B   *A doesn't like snakes, and I don't like spinach.*
  PUPIL C   *A doesn't like snakes, B doesn't like spinach, and I don't like horror films.*
  PUPIL D   *A doesn't like snakes . . .*

If you don't know the words, ask your teacher.

11 Do you like swimming? Present simple in yes/no questions

Do you **like** swimming, Jenny?
Yes, I **do**.

Does Nick **like** swimming?
Yes, he **does**. Very much.

And what about Trig?
Does he **like** swimming?
No, he **doesn't**.
He **doesn't like** water!

Oh yes, I **do**!

Grammar lesson

Present simple in yes/no questions

Do with   **Does** with
I, **you**, **we** and **they**   **he**, **she** and **it**

Do $\left\{\begin{array}{c} I \\ you \\ we \\ they \end{array}\right\}$ **like?**   **Does** $\left\{\begin{array}{c} he \\ she \\ it \end{array}\right\}$ **like?**

Short answers

Do you like fizzy drinks?
Yes, I do.

Does Chip like fizzy drinks?
Yes, he does.

Does Trig like fizzy drinks?
No, he doesn't.

Stupid! **Yes, I do.**

1 What do they do?

Put in **Do** or **Does**.

► _Do_____ Nick and Jenny get up early?

► _Does_____ Trig like fizzy drinks?

1 _____ the children walk to school?

2 _____ lessons start at nine o'clock?

3 _____ Trig go to school?

4 _____ Jenny like school?

5 _____ Nick like school?

6 _____ they have lunch at school?

7 _____ lessons finish at three thirty
every day?

8 _____ Trig play games?

9 _____ the children watch television in
the evenings?

10 _____ Trig watch space films on
television?

11 _____ he go to bed at nine o'clock?

12 _____ Nick and Jenny go to bed at
nine o'clock?

13 _____ they read comics in bed?

14 _____ they go to sleep at nine thirty?

15 _____ Trig go to sleep at nine o'clock?

16 _____ he read comics?

2 A questionnaire

Make a questionnaire about hobbies and interests. Begin with **Do you** . . . ?

Here are some ideas. Ask about:

Sports
swimming, football, tennis, basketball

Collecting
stamps, posters, stickers

Musical instruments
the piano, the guitar, the violin

Activities at home
television, radio, records, books, comics

Places to go
the cinema, the theatre, the park

```
Questionnnaire

Sports                      yes    no
Do you go swimming?          ✔     ___
Do you play football?       ___     ✔

Collecting
Do you collect stamps?      ___     ✔

Musical instruments
Do you play the piano?       ✔     ___
```

Now ask your partner the questions.

3 About you

Give short answers.

▶ Do you like dogs?   *Yes, I do.*
▶ Do you like snails?   *No, I don't.*

1 Do you like cats?
2 Do you play football?
3 Do you watch space films on television?
4 Do you play computer games?
5 Do you buy chewing gum?
6 Do you go to bed late?
7 Do you spend pocket money on sweets?
8 Do you like horror films?
9 Do you help with the housework?
10 Do you wear glasses?
11 Do you go to sleep in lessons?
12 Do you ride a bicycle?
13 Do you keep a pet?
14 Do you like spiders?

4 Do they like these things?

Ask questions round the class.

▶ PUPIL A   *Does Jenny like milk-shakes?*
  PUPIL B   *Yes, she does.*
  PUPIL C   *Does Nick like peanuts?*
  PUPIL D   *No, he doesn't.*

Jenny ☺ milk-shakes, pizza, fizzy drinks, chocolate, sweets

☹ chewing gum, popcorn, crisps, peanuts

Nick ☺ popcorn, chewing gum, chocolate, Coke

☹ peanuts, pizza, crisps, sweets, ice-lollies

5 Class game: guessing jobs

Here are sixteen jobs.

waiter/waitress	secretary	architect
shop assistant	electrician	teacher
TV newsreader	carpenter	doctor
policeman	mechanic	pilot
hairdresser	bus driver	farmer
nurse		

Play the game like this:

a. Choose a job from the list. Mime an action from the job.
b. The class asks questions about the job with *Do you* . . . ?
c. Answer: *Yes, I do.* OR *No, I don't.*
d. After six questions, the class guesses your job: *Are you a/an* . . . ?

Here are some useful questions:

Do you work with other people?
Do you work indoors/outdoors?
Do you work in an office?
Do you work at night?
Do you help people?
Do you repair things?
Do you use languages?
Do you travel?

Write more questions before you start the game.

12 What do you do?

MR BELL   TOM

Do you play a game, Tom?

Yes, of course.

What do you play?

Football. I'm in the school team.

When do you practise?

On Tuesdays and Fridays.
In the afternoon.
At four o'clock.

Where do you practise?

At school. Outside **in** summer and in the gymnasium **in** winter.

When's the next school match?

In June.
On the tenth.

Good luck.

Thanks!

Grammar lesson

Questions with **what** etc.

Some question words:

what	**who**
what time	**why**
when	**how**
where	**how often**

		Subject	
	Does	Tom	play a game?
What	does	he	play?
When	does	he	practise?
Where	does	he	practise?
When	is	the next match?	

Prepositions of time

in	a month	**in June**
	a year	**in 1995**
	a season	**in winter, in summer**
	a time of day	**in the afternoon(s)**
		in the evening(s)
on	a day	**on Tuesday(s)**
		on Saturday afternoon(s)
	a date	**on the tenth (of June)**
at	a clock-time	**at four o'clock**
	a special time of the year	**at Christmas, at Easter**

1 What's wrong?

Trig wants to write some sentences with question words, but they are mixed up.

Please help!

▶ | do | What | play | you | ?

What do you play?

1 | do | When | play | you | ?

_____

2 | you | Where | practise | do | ?

_____

3 | How often | play | do | you | ?

_____

4 | When | the | team | does | practise | ?

_____

5 | you | do | like | football | Why | ?

_____

6 | is | the | When | next | game | ?

_____

7 | What time | does | start | it | ?

_____

8 | finish | it | does | When | ?

_____

9 | Tom | does | play | How often | ?

_____

10 | play | he | does | Where | ?

_____

2 Questions, questions, questions!

Complete the questions with **Where**, **When**, **What**, **How**.

▶ _Where_ do you live?

1 _____ do you get up?

2 _____ do you have for breakfast?

3 _____ do you leave home?

4 _____ do you go to school?
By bicycle or by bus?

5 _____ do lessons start?

6 _____ do you have lunch?
At home or at school?

7 _____ do you like best at school?
Games?

8 _____ do you go after school?

9 _____ do you do your homework?
Before or after supper?

10 _____ do you do on Saturday
and Sunday?

11 _____ do you have holidays?

12 _____ do you wear to school?

13 _____ do you wear for games?

14 _____ do you carry your books
to school? In a school bag?

15 _____ do you want for your
birthday?

Now ask a partner these questions.

3 Free time activities

A friend does these things. You want to know more. Ask questions with question words.

▶ I watch television. (When)
 When do you watch it?

1 I read comics. (How often)
2 I play games. (What)
3 I go out at the weekend. (Where)
4 I swim at the pool. (What time)
5 I collect things. (What)
6 I write to pen-friends. (How often)
7 I play football. (Where)

8 I take my sister to school. (What time)
9 I go to a sports club. (When)
10 I watch cartoons on television. (When)
11 I take my dog for a walk. (When)
12 I go to a youth club. (How often)
13 I go to piano lessons. (What time)
14 I go shopping. (Where)

---

4 About Tom

a Complete the sentences with **in**, **on** or **at**.

At school Tom likes Games best. That's ▶ *on* Tuesdays and Fridays
▶ *at* two o'clock. ¹_____ Mondays, Wednesdays and Thursdays
he's glad when school finishes ²_____ three thirty.

He hates Maths because the teacher gives homework every day.
He does the homework in the bus on the way to school!

There is no school ³_____ Saturdays, so ⁴_____ the afternoon
he goes swimming with his friends. ⁵_____ the evening he watches
television or plays with his model railway.

He likes the long school holidays ⁶_____ summer and
the holidays ⁷_____ Christmas and Easter. His birthday
is ⁸_____ December ⁹_____ the twenty-fifth. So he gets
a lot of presents ¹⁰_____ Christmas.

b Now answer these questions about Tom.
1 What does he like best at school?
2 When does he have Games?
3 Why does he hate Maths?
4 Where does he do his Maths homework?
5 When does school finish?
6 Where does he go on Saturday afternoons?

7 When does he play with his model railway?
8 When are the school holidays?
9 When is his birthday?
10 Why does he get a lot of presents at Christmas?

5 Favourite television programmes

a Look at the list of television programmes and answer the questions.

Children's programmes 10–15 September

Monday

5.00	Animal World
6.00	Cartoon Time
7.00	Galaxies
7.30	Young Detectives

Tuesday

4.30	The Last Frontier
5.00	Video Club
6.00	Walton Road
6.30	Freddy

Wednesday

4.30	What's Next
5.30	The Martins
6.00	Cartoon Time
7.00	Seven Seas

Thursday

4.30	The Last Frontier
5.00	Animal World
6.00	Ghost Train
6.30	Freddy

Friday

5.00	Video Club
6.00	Laserman
6.30	School's Out
7.30	Friday Cinema

Saturday

12.00	Junior Scientist
1.00	Questions and Answers
1.30	Sports World
2.30	Space 4000

▶ When is Animal World?
Animal World is on Mondays and Thursdays at five o'clock.

1 When is Sports World?
2 When is Galaxies?
3 When is The Last Frontier?
4 When is Cartoon Time?
5 When is Friday Cinema?
6 When is Space 4000?
7 When is Young Detectives?
8 When is What's Next?
9 When is Video Club?
10 When is Seven Seas?
11 When is Questions and Answers?
12 When is Freddy?
13 When is The Martins?
14 When is Laserman?
15 When is School's Out?
16 When is Walton Road?
17 When is Junior Scientist?
18 When is Ghost Train?

b Ask three pupils in the class about their favourite television programmes, like this:

▶ YOU *When is your favourite television programme?*
PUPIL *It's on Wednesdays at seven o'clock.*

13 Slow down, Trig — Imperatives

Slow down, Trig.
Don't go so fast.

Don't fall.
Be careful!

Look out!
Jump off
the skateboard.

Don't hit the dustb . . .

Oh dear. Too late . . .
Poor Trig . . .

. . . and poor dustbin!

Grammar lesson

Imperatives

Affirmative	*Negative*
Verb only	**Don't** OR **Do not** + verb
Slow down.	**Don't go** so fast.
Look out!	**Don't fall.**
Be careful!	**Don't hit** the dustbin.

Use imperatives for orders, warnings,
instructions and advice.

---

1 What do they say?

Your teacher   Your mother

Say what your mother or teacher says, like
this:

▶ You don't drink your milk.
   My mother says, 'Drink your milk.'

▶ You talk in class.
   My teacher says, 'Don't talk in class.'

1   You don't get up.
2   You eat chocolate before lunch.
3   You don't clean your teeth.
4   You make a noise in class.
5   You don't wash your hands before meals.
6   You don't eat your vegetables.
7   You play loud music on the radio.
8   You eat your lunch in class.
9   You don't help with the washing up.
10 You don't tidy your room.
11 You read comics in class.
12 You jump on your bed.
13 You don't do your English exercises.
14 You don't go to bed.
15 You play ball in the kitchen.
16 You don't make your bed.
17 You fight in class.
18 You sleep in class.
19 You don't feed the goldfish.
20 You whistle in class.
21 You write letters in class.
22 You make paper aeroplanes in class.
23 You don't have a bath.
24 You hit your brother.
25 You watch television all day.

2 Class instructions

Complete the teacher's instructions with these verbs and **Don't**, where necessary. Sometimes two or three verbs are possible.

Use:

answer	find	make	speak
close ✓	go	open	stand
come	learn	play	talk ✓
disturb	listen	read	work
eat	look	sit	write

▶ *Don't talk* _____ in class.

▶ *Close* _____ your books.

1 _____ in pairs.

2 _____ your books at page 12.

3 _____ sweets in class.

4 _____ at your neighbour's book.

5 _____ with a partner.

6 _____ to the blackboard.

7 _____ sentences with these words.

8 _____ out of the window.

9 _____ the questions.

10 _____ down the answer.

11 _____ this game.

12 _____ the missing words.

13 _____ to the cassette.

14 _____ down.

15 _____ up.

16 _____ these new words.

17 _____ the other pupils.

18 _____ two teams.

19 _____ English.

20 _____ so much noise.

3 Signs

Say what the signs mean.
Use these verbs with or without **Don't**:

drink	light fires	turn right ✓
drop litter	overtake	go straight on
go	smoke	pick flowers
park	touch	play music
stop ✓	turn left	take photographs
talk		

▶ 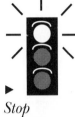 *Stop*

▶  *Don't turn right.*

1

8

2

9 silence

3

10

4

11

5

12

6

13

7

14

14 What is there in Merton? there is/are; Prepositions of place

There's a school **in** Park Street.

Next to the school **there's** a small park.
There are trees and flowers **in** the park,
and **there's** also a children's playground.

There are two supermarkets and some
other shops. **Behind** the shops **there's**
a library. It's **between** the post office
and the bank.

Is there a cinema, Jenny?

No, **there isn't.**

Are there many cafés
with banana milk-shakes?

Grammar lesson

there is/are

Singular
There is a school in Park Street.
There's a park next to the school.
There isn't a cinema.

Plural
There are some supermarkets and restaurants.
There aren't many cafés.

Questions
Is there a cinema?
Are there many shops?

Short answers
Yes, there is. **No, there isn't.**
Yes, there are. **No, there aren't.**

Prepositions of place

Where's Trig?

He's **in** the box.

He's **on** the box.

He's **next to** the box.

He's **between** two boxes.

He's **behind** the box.

He's **under** the box.

1 Merton

Look at the map of Merton again.
Put in **there's**, **there isn't**, **there are**, **there aren't**, **is there** or **are there**.

▶ <u>There's</u> a school in Park Street, and next to the school [1]_____ a small park.

In the park [2]_____ a children's playground.

[3]_____ two supermarkets and many other shops.

[4]_____ a post office and [5]_____ a library, too.

[6]_____ some restaurants, but [7]_____ many cafés.

Unfortunately, [8]_____ a cinema. [9]_____ a sports centre?

No, [10]_____, but [11]_____ a football pitch in the park.

How many cinemas [12]_____ in your town? How many schools [13]_____?
[14]_____ a supermarket?

2 Littletown

Look at this street map of Littletown, near Merton.

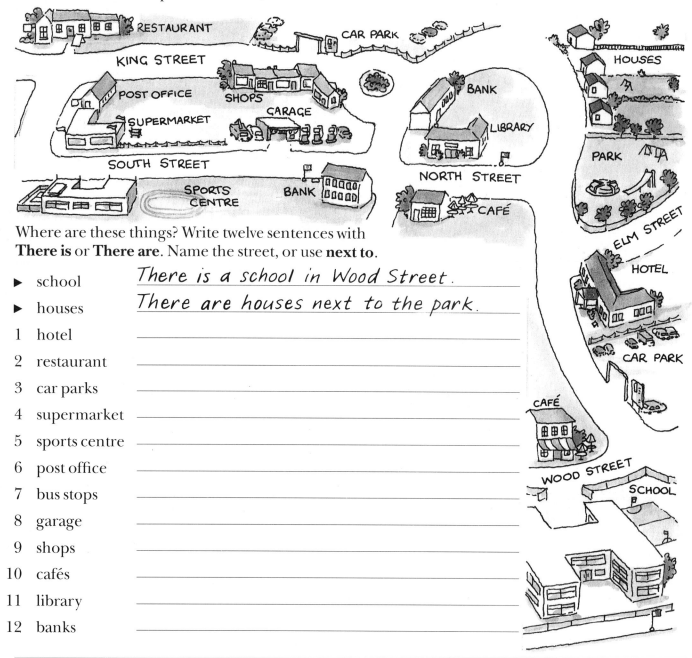

Where are these things? Write twelve sentences with
There is or **There are**. Name the street, or use **next to**.

▶ school   *There is a school in Wood Street.*

▶ houses   *There are houses next to the park.*

1 hotel _____

2 restaurant _____

3 car parks _____

4 supermarket _____

5 sports centre _____

6 post office _____

7 bus stops _____

8 garage _____

9 shops _____

10 cafés _____

11 library _____

12 banks _____

3 Where you live

Answer the questions.
Say **Yes, there is/are.** OR **No, there isn't/aren't**.

1 Is there a cinema in your town?
2 Is there a park near your home?
3 Are there many shops near your home?
4 Is there a sports centre in your town?
5 Is there a bus stop in your street?
6 Are there many blocks of flats in your town?
7 Is there a telephone box in your street?

8 Are there many trees in your street?
9 Are there many office blocks in your town?
10 Is there a children's playground near your home?
11 Are there many restaurants in your town?
12 Are there many cafés in your town?

4 Where are Nick's things?

Look at this untidy room. It's Nick's room.

Write where these things are.

Use:

▶ His socks *are on the lamp.*

▶ His comics *are on the floor under the desk.*

1 His books _____

2 His guitar _____

3 His skateboard _____

4 His keys _____

5 His alarm clock _____

6 His tennis racket _____

7 His shoes _____

8 His suitcase _____

9 His school bag _____

10 His cap and scarf _____

11 His jacket _____

12 His radio _____

in
on
next to
between
behind
under

basket
bed
chair
cupboard
desk
doorknob
floor
lamp

5 Memory game

Look at the picture of Nick's room again for one minute.
Cover the picture. Answer these questions.

▶ Where are his socks? *They're on the lamp.*
▶ Where's his suitcase? *It's on the floor between the bed and the cupboard.*

1 Where's Nick's school bag?
2 Where's his tennis racket?
3 Where are his comics?
4 Where's his radio?

5 Where are his cap and scarf?
6 Where's his jacket?
7 Where are his books?

8 Where's his skateboard?
9 Where's his guitar?
10 Where are his keys?

15 Can he speak English?   **can** for ability

Can Trig understand English?

Yes, he **can** understand quite a lot. He's clever.

Can he speak English?

No, he **can't**. Not yet.

Oh yes, **I can**!

Can you understand Trig's language?

Oh no, we **can't**.
Not a word!

Grammar lesson

can for ability

I		I	
you		you	
he		he	
she	**can**	she	**cannot** OR
it		it	**can't**
we		we	
you		you	
they		they	

Questions
Can I?
Can he?

Short answers
Can you speak English? **Yes, I can.**
Can Trig speak English? **No, he can't.**
Can you speak his language? **No, we can't.**

1 Things you can do

Say what you **can** and **cannot** (or **can't**) do.
Make eight sentences.

▶ *I can speak English but I can't speak French.*
▶ *I can play football and I can play table tennis.*

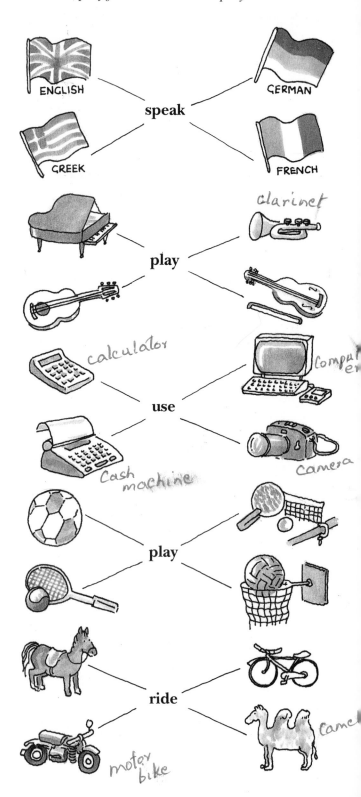

2 Can elephants fly?

Which is right and which is wrong?
Write sentences. Use **can** or **can't**.

▶ Elephants can fly.
   <u>Wrong. Elephants can't fly.</u>

▶ Dogs can swim.
   <u>Right. Dogs can swim.</u>

1 Penguins can swim.
   _____

2 Penguins can fly.
   _____

3 Horses can swim.
   _____

4 Lions can climb trees.
   _____

5 Elephants can catch fish.
   _____

6 Dogs can climb trees.
   _____

7 Parrots can fly.
   _____

8 Cats can fly.
   _____

9 Camels can run.
   _____

10 Bears can catch fish.
   _____

11 Spiders can swim.
   _____

12 Sheep can jump.
   _____

3 What can they do?

a Say what they **can** and **cannot** (or **can't**) do, like this:

▶ *Jenny, Nick and Tom can swim under water.*
  Amanda can't.

b Now work with a partner. Ask questions and give short answers.

▶ YOU   *Can you swim under water?*
  PARTNER   *Yes, I can.* OR *No, I can't.*

Can they . . .	Jenny	Nick	Tom	Amanda
▶ swim under water?	✓	✓	✓	✗
1 dive?	✓	✓	✗	✓
2 put up a tent?	✗	✓	✗	✓
3 row a boat?	✗	✓	✓	✓
4 make a camp fire?	✗	✓	✗	✓
5 sew on a button?	✓	✗	✗	✓
6 make an omelette?	✓	✗	✓	✗
7 tie knots?	✗	✓	✓	✓
8 do first aid?	✓	✓	✗	✓
9 climb a rope?	✗	✓	✓	✓
10 read a map?	✓	✗	✓	✓

No, I can't . . .

16 Trig is helping   Present continuous

It's Saturday afternoon. What **are** the Bells **doing**? **Are** they **working**?

The sun**'s shining**. Mrs Bell **is hanging** the clothes on the line.

It **isn't raining** today, so Mr Bell **is digging** in the garden.

Chip**'s having** fun. At the moment he**'s running** after the neighbours' cat.

Jenny and Nick **are washing** the dishes in the kitchen.

And what**'s** Trig **doing** now?
Oh, dear! He**'s helping**!
He**'s hanging** the dishes on the line . . .

Grammar lesson

Present continuous

Make the **ing** form with the verb + **ing** :
do → do**ing**, work → work**ing**,
help → help**ing**.

But
1 take away a final **e**:
   shin**e** → shining, hav**e** → having

2 after one vowel + one consonant,
   double the consonant:
   dig → di**gg**ing, run → ru**nn**ing

Use **be** + **ing** form for the present continuous.

Long forms		*Short forms*	
I **am**		I**'m**	
you **are**		you**'re**	
he **is**		he**'s**	
she **is**		she**'s**	
it **is**	working	it**'s**	working
we **are**		we**'re**	
you **are**		you**'re**	
they **are**		they**'re**	

I am **not working**   I**'m not working**
you **are not working**   you **aren't working**
he **is not working**   he **isn't working**

Questions
Am I **working**?
Are you **working**?
Is he **working**?

Short answers
Are you working?   **Yes, I am.**
Is she working?   **No, she isn't.**
Are they working?   **No, they aren't.**

Use the present continuous for something that is happening now. Often with **now, at the moment, today.**

1 What is he writing?

Trig is writing **ing** forms, but what a mess!

Help him, like this:

- ▶ wash *washing*
- ▶ write *writing*
- ▶ run *running*
- 1 have _____
- 2 swim _____
- 3 take _____
- 4 stop _____
- 5 fly _____
- 6 speak _____
- 7 use _____
- 8 make _____

- 9 eat _____
- 10 help _____
- 11 put _____
- 12 read _____
- 13 get _____
- 14 watch _____
- 15 come _____
- 16 learn _____
- 17 catch _____
- 18 sit _____
- 19 rain _____

- 20 hit _____
- 21 look _____
- 22 go _____
- 23 drop _____
- 24 chase _____
- 25 walk _____
- 26 bake _____
- 27 kick _____
- 28 clap _____
- 29 carry _____
- 30 give _____

2 At home with the Bells

Put in the **ing** forms.

The Bells are at home today. It isn't ▶ *raining* _____ .

The sun's [1] _____ , so

Mrs Bell is [2] _____ the clothes on the line.

The children are [3] _____ the dishes.

Mr Bell is [4] _____ in the garden.

What's Chip [5] _____ now?

Oh, dear! He's [6] _____ after the neighbours' cat.

And what's Trig [7] _____ ? Oh, no! He's [8] _____ !

He's [9] _____ the dishes on the line.

3   What are they doing now?

It's Sunday afternoon. The Allens are visiting the Bells.

a   Say and write what they are doing.

Use:

drink	look	sit
eat	play	sleep
have	run	stand
hide	shout ✓	talk (x 2)

Jenny ▶*is shouting* _____ at Chip!

Mrs Allen ¹_____ under the big tree. She ²_____ to Mrs Bell.

They ³_____ tea. Nick ⁴_____ ball with Tom.

Tom ⁵_____ a sandwich.

Chip ⁶_____ fun. He ⁷_____ round the garden again.

The neighbours' cat ⁸_____ behind a bush.

Mr Bell ⁹_____ to Mr Allen. They ¹⁰_____ next to

the flower bed. They ¹¹_____ at the roses.

Trig ¹²_____ in the tree.

b   Now answer these questions.

▶   Is Jenny hiding? *No, she isn't. She's shouting.*

1   Are Mrs Allen and Mrs Bell standing?
2   Is Chip sleeping?
3   Are Nick and Tom sitting under the tree?
4   Is the cat running round the garden?
5   Is Trig eating a sandwich?
6   Are Mr Bell and Mr Allen playing ball?
7   Is Tom drinking tea?

4 Trig's first football match

Trig is watching his first football match with Tom.
Trig doesn't understand what is happening.
Help him to make questions with **Why**.
Use words from each box.

Why	

is
are

they
he
she

running?
holding the ball? ✓
kicking the ball?
shouting?
jumping up and down?
blowing the whistle?
sleeping?
hitting the ball with his head?
clapping?
singing?
carrying a player?

▶ *Why is he holding the ball?*

5

1

6

2

7

3

8

4

9

10

5 Miming game

Think of an action (for example, opening or closing a window).
Mime the action in front of the class.
The class now asks questions and you answer like this:

▶ CLASS   *Are you cleaning something?*
    YOU   *No, I'm not.*
    CLASS   *Are you playing a game?*
    YOU   *No, I'm not.*
    CLASS   *Are you opening a window?*
    YOU   *Yes, I am.*

Here are some ideas:

playing table tennis/basketball
cleaning your bicycle/shoes/the carpet/
    the windows
writing a letter
doing your homework
making your bed/a cake
drawing/painting a picture

Object pronouns; **like**, **love**, **hate** + **ing** form

Trig and Chip **love hiding**. Can you see **them**?

Grammar lesson

Object pronouns

Subject pronouns	Object pronouns
I	me
you	you
he	him
she	her
it	it
we	us
you	you
they	them

Use object pronouns after verbs and after prepositions.

▶ *I can't see **him**.*   *I hate looking for **them**.*
  *Ask **her**.*   *Take the ball with **you**.*

like, love, hate + ing form

We often use the **ing** form after **like**, **love** and **hate**.

▶ *Chip **likes chasing** the cat next door.*
*Chip and Trig **love hiding**.*
*Nick **hates doing** homework.*

1 Missing things

Put in **me**, **you**, **him**, **her**, **it**, **us** or **them**.

JENNY   I can't find my coloured pencils. Have you got ▶ *them* ?

NICK   No, I haven't. And my cap is missing. Can you see ¹_____ ?

JENNY   Sorry, no, I can't. Amanda's waiting for ²_____ downstairs.

Tell ³_____ I'm looking for my pencils.

NICK   Stupid cap! Who's got ⁴_____ ? I'm late for school again.

Help ⁵_____ , Jenny!

JENNY   I can't help ⁶_____ . I'm looking for my pencils. Can you see ⁷_____ ?

Oh, no, my school bag's missing as well! Are you hiding ⁸_____ ?

NICK   No, I'm not!

JENNY   You're lying. Give it to ⁹_____ .

NICK   I'm telling ¹⁰_____ the truth!

JENNY   Well, Mum's in the kitchen. Ask ¹¹_____ .

Perhaps she can tell ¹²_____ where our things are.

NICK   By the way, where's Trig? Can you see ¹³_____ ?

Where are the missing things? Do you know who's got ¹⁴_____ ?

---

2 Jenny's list

Look at Jenny's list and answer the
questions with **him**, **her**, **it** or **them**.

▶ Does she like the headmaster?
Yes, she likes him.
▶ Does she like Jill and Ben Potter?
No, she doesn't like them.

1 Does she like Ann Fox?
2 Does she like John Green?
3 Does she like school meals?
4 Does she like Miss Mill?
5 Does she like History?
6 Does she like exams?
7 Does she like the Walker twins?
8 Does she like Mr Barker?
9 Does she like Kate Robbins?
10 Does she like Jimmy Leech?
11 Does she like English?
12 Does she like Art?

Do **you** like English?

Jenny Bell At School.

I like ☺	I don't like ☹
Art	exams
English	History
Miss Mill	Mr Barker
Ann Fox	John Green
The Walker twins	Jill and Ben Potter
the headmaster	school meals
Jimmy Leech	Kate Robbins

3 Sports

a Here is a list of Nick's sports favourites.
Tom likes (✓) some of them but doesn't like (✗) others.

	NICK	TOM
female sports star	Steffi Graf	✓
male sports star	Carl Lewis	✗
sports team	Manchester United	✗
team sport	football	✓
individual sport	golf	✗
sports cars	Ferraris	✓

Make sentences about Tom and Nick like this:

▶ *Nick likes Steffi Graf and Tom likes her too.*
▶ *Nick likes Carl Lewis but Tom doesn't like him.*

b Make your own list and exchange it with your partner.

Your name: _____   Your partner's name: _____

female sports star	
male sports star	
sports team	
team sport	
individual sport	
sports cars	

Then write sentences like this:

▶ I like Steffi Graf and Tom likes her too.
▶ I like Carl Lewis but Tom doesn't like him.

1 _____
2 _____
3 _____
4 _____
5 _____
6 _____

4 In your free time

Write true sentences about yourself with
like, **love** or **hate**.

▶ drawing
I like drawing.

1 swimming

_____

2 running

_____

3 going to the theatre

_____

4 dancing

_____

5 shopping

_____

6 learning poetry

_____

7 playing the piano

_____

8 painting

_____

9 watching television

_____

10 singing

_____

11 reading science fiction

_____

12 going to pop concerts

_____

13 visiting museums

_____

14 cooking

_____

15 playing football

_____

5 What do you like?

Work with a partner.
Ask your partner if he or she likes doing
these things. Answer with **love** or **hate**.

▶ playing tennis
YOU   *Do you like playing tennis?*
PARTNER   *Yes, I love playing tennis.* OR
           No, I hate playing tennis.

1 doing Maths homework
2 travelling
3 camping
4 buying clothes
5 babysitting
6 having your hair cut
7 going to the dentist
8 taking medicine
9 staying up late
10 getting up early
11 fighting
12 cleaning your shoes
13 going on holiday
14 tidying your room
15 speaking English
16 shopping for food
17 telephoning
18 writing letters
19 cleaning your teeth
20 eating in restaurants

18 I can, but you mustn't · can for permission; must for necessity

Grammar lesson

can for permission

▶ *Can I go to the cinema?*
No, you can't.

Can Tom come this afternoon?
Yes, he can.

Can he stay till midnight?
No, he can't!

must for necessity

I you he she it we you they	must	I you he she it we you they	must not OR mustn't

No **s** with he/she/it.
No **to** after **must**.

▶ *I've got a cold. I must stay in bed today.*
You must tidy your room.

I mustn't forget to tidy my room.
You mustn't go out with a cold.

1 Can you or can't you?

Ask permission with **Can I . . . ?**
Then give the probable answer.

You want to . . .

▶ . . . go to see a horror film.
Ask your father.
Can I go to see a horror film?
No, you can't!

1 . . . invite ten friends to lunch.
Ask your mother.
2 . . . go camping in the woods.
Ask your mother.
3 . . . have some extra English homework.
Ask your teacher.
4 . . . eat sweets in bed.
Ask your dentist.
5 . . . cook lunch on Sunday.
Ask your mother.
6 . . . go swimming with a bad cold.
Ask your doctor.
7 . . . wash the car.
Ask your father.
8 . . . have more pocket money.
Ask your mother.
9 . . . watch television until midnight.
Ask your father.
10 . . . do this exercise again.
Ask your teacher.

2 Ask your partner

You want to borrow some things from your partner. Ask him or her, like this:

▶ pencil

YOU   *Can I borrow your pencil, please?*
PARTNER   *Yes, you can.* OR *No, you can't.*

1	ruler	7	dictionary
2	pen	8	felt pen
3	rubber	9	coursebook
4	pencil sharpener	10	sticky tape
5	scissors	11	atlas
6	grammar book	12	glue

3 Classroom rules

Put in **We must** or **We mustn't**.
Make true sentences.

▶ *We must* _____ sit still.
▶ *We mustn't* _____ jump on the desks.

1 _____ fight.
2 _____ do what the teacher says.
3 _____ go to sleep.
4 _____ be quiet.
5 _____ play football.
6 _____ look at the blackboard.
7 _____ eat crisps.
8 _____ draw on the desks.
9 _____ listen to the teacher.
10 _____ give answers.
11 _____ read comics.
12 _____ make a lot of noise.
13 _____ look at the teacher.
14 _____ jump out of the windows.
15 _____ listen to Walkmans.
16 _____ write letters to friends.

4 Necessity

Put in **must** or **mustn't**.

▶ Trig, you *mustn't* _____ squirt your water pistol at people.

1 It's a secret. You _____ tell Jenny or Amanda.
2 Shhh. Dad's asleep. We _____ be quiet.
3 Nick, you _____ spend all your pocket money at once.
4 We _____ write to Grandmother. It's her birthday tomorrow.
5 Trig, you _____ squirt toothpaste at Chip.
6 I _____ forget my homework again. Mr Blake gets angry.
7 You _____ eat so much, Trig. You are too fat.
8 Chip, you _____ chase Fluff. She's a sweet little cat.
9 You really _____ tidy your room, Nick. I can't open the door!
10 Chip, you _____ tear the postman's trousers.
11 Chip, you _____ bury your bones in the flower beds.
12 It's six o'clock. I _____ go home now, Jenny.
13 Nick, you _____ say 'Shut up' to adults.
14 Trig, you _____ learn some new English words every day.
15 Trig, you're dirty. You really _____ have a bath!

19 How much milk? some, any; how much, how many

Nick and Jenny want to make a cake for their school party.

JENNY We need **some** sugar, **some** flour, **some** eggs, **some** butter and **some** milk.

NICK Milk? We haven't got **any**! **How much** milk?

JENNY Not much. But we can use water.

NICK Well, at least we've got **some** water! And **how many** eggs do we need? Have we got **any**? Where are they?

Ask Trig!

Grammar lesson

some and any

1 Use **some** and **any** with plurals and with uncountable nouns.
   ▶ *We've got **some** lemons.*
      *We've got **some** butter.*
      *We haven't got **any** eggs.*
      *We haven't got **any** milk.*
      *Have we got **any** apples?*
      *Have we got **any** sugar?*

2 Use **some** in affirmative sentences.
   ▶ *We need **some** eggs.*
      *We've got **some** water.*

3 Use **any** in negative sentences.
   ▶ *We haven't got **any** eggs.*
      *There isn't **any** milk.*

4 Use **any** in most questions.
   ▶ *Are there **any** eggs?*
      *Have we got **any** milk?*

how much and how many

1 Use **how much** with uncountable nouns.
   ▶ *How much milk have we got?*
      How much flour is there?

2 Use **how many** with countable nouns.
   ▶ *How many eggs have we got?*
      How many lemons are there?

1 Making a cake

Put in **some** or **any**.

Jenny and Nick want to make a chocolate cake. They've got ▶ *Some* flour.

Is there 1_____ margarine or butter, Nick?

There isn't 2_____ margarine, but there's 3_____ butter in the fridge.

They've got 4_____ sugar, but what else do they need? Well, they need 5_____ eggs and 6_____ milk. Unfortunately, they haven't got 7_____ milk, but at least they've got 8_____ water! And have they got 9_____ cocoa? Oh, dear. There isn't 10_____ .

---

2 Memory game

Look at the things on the kitchen table for one minute. Close the book.
Name what's on the table. Use **a**, **an** or **some**.

▶ *some meat, a banana, some cherries . . .*

3 Is there any?

Look at the picture in Exercise 2 again.
Ask a partner questions with **any**.
The partner answers with **some** or **any**, like this:

▶ rice?

YOU　　　　*Is there any rice?*
PARTNER　*Yes, there's some rice.*

▶ oranges?

YOU　　　　*Are there any oranges?*
PARTNER　*No, there aren't any oranges.*

1	coffee?	9	tomatoes?
2	bread?	10	tea?
3	cheese?	11	flour?
4	apples?	12	chocolate?
5	orange juice?	13	cherries?
6	potatoes?	14	sugar?
7	milk?	15	grapes?
8	meat?	16	dates?

4 More cooking

You want to make these things.
Write what you need and what you don't need.
Use **some** and **any**.

 ▶ vegetable soup

I need some onions, some salt, some carrots and some peas. I don't need any pineapples or any peaches.

 1 strawberry jam

_____

_____

 2 a cheese omelette

_____

_____

 3 a lemon cake

_____

_____

 4 a cup of tea

_____

_____

 5 a banana milk-shake

_____

_____

5 Interview

Ask a partner some questions.
Begin them with **How much** or **How many**.

▶ pocket money do you get every week?
How much pocket money do you get every week?
▶ brothers and sisters have you got?
How many brothers and sisters have you got?

1 money do you spend every week?
2 comics do you buy in a year?
3 money do you save every week?
4 sweets do you buy every week?
5 chocolate do you eat every week?
6 milk or cocoa do you drink every day?
7 pets have you got?
8 pen-friends have you got?
9 letters do you write every week?
10 time do you spend on homework every day?

6 Puzzle

Complete the sentences to solve the puzzle.

Across

1 How ▶ _many_ books have you got?

4 They are poor. They haven't got much _____ .

5 We need some _____ to make a pizza.

7 I want some fruit. Have you got any _____ ?

10 Nick's got a toffee and a bar of chocolate but Jenny hasn't got any _____ .

12 How much _____ do you drink every day?

Down

1 How _____ rain falls in England every year?

2 He is hungry. He wants _____ bread.

3 She is late. She hasn't got much _____ .

6 We haven't got any _____ We can't make an omelette.

8 They haven't got _____ stamps. I can't post my letter.

9 I always like some _____ in my coffee.

11 Jenny is thirsty. She wants some _____

20 How often do you help? Adverbs of frequency

AMANDA How **often** do you help in the house, Nick?

NICK Oh, I **often** do things. I tidy my room **three times a week**.

JENNY That's a lie. You **never** tidy your room. You are **always** too busy. Mum does it **every Monday**.

NICK That's not fair, Jenny! I **sometimes** do it – at least **twice a year**.

Grammar lesson

Adverbs of frequency

Adverbs of frequency tell us how often something happens.

---

never, often, always etc.

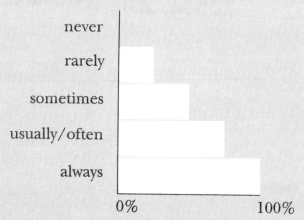

We put **never, often, always** etc.

1 before a full verb:
   ▶ You **never** tidy your room.
   I **often** do things in the house.
   Mum **always** does it.

2 after the verb **be**:
   ▶ You are **always** too busy!

---

once a week, every Monday etc.

How often do you tidy your room?
once a week
twice a week
three times a week
every Monday

Also: **once an hour/a month/a year;
every morning/night/year/Christmas** etc.

Look where they usually stand in the sentence.
▶ I tidy my room **once a week**.
Mum tidies your room **every Monday**.

1 Tell the truth!

Put in **never**, **rarely**, **sometimes**, **usually**, **often** or **always**.

▶ I [never] do bad things!

Oh, Trig! Are you telling the truth?

1 I _____ lose things.
2 I _____ do my English homework.
3 I _____ borrow money.
4 I _____ break things.
5 I _____ fight.
6 I _____ help my parents.
7 I _____ make a mess in my room.
8 I _____ spend all my pocket money.
9 I _____ go to bed late.
10 I _____ tell the truth.

2 Tell the truth – again!

Write the sentences, putting in **never**, **rarely**, **sometimes**, **usually**, **often** or **always**.

▶ I eat sweets.
I never eat sweets.

Trig? Are you sure?

Oh, all right!

I often eat sweets.

1 I read comics in bed. _____

2 We go camping at weekends. _____

3 I buy chewing gum. _____

4 We go to the zoo. _____

5 I buy cassettes. _____

6 I go to pop concerts. _____

7 We get up at six on Sundays. _____

8 I play basketball. _____

9 I forget things. _____

10 We watch television. _____

3 Holidays

Copy the sentences but put in the words in brackets ().

▶ The Bells go on holiday in August. (always) *The Bells always go on holiday in August.*

▶ The weather is good. (usually) *The weather is usually good.*

1 They stay in England. (rarely) _____

2 They drive to Scotland or Wales. (sometimes) _____

3 In August there is a lot of traffic on the roads. (often) _____

4 They go to Greece or Spain. (sometimes) _____

5 In August the weather is wonderful there. (usually) _____

6 They take the car abroad. (never) _____

7 Before the holidays Nick and Jenny are excited. (always) _____

8 Chip goes with them to Scotland or Wales. (always) _____

9 When they go abroad, he stays with the Allens or with the Todds. (usually) _____

10 But unfortunately he isn't a good dog. (always) _____

4 How often do you . . . ?

Write answers to these questions. Use:

once (or **twice** or **three times**) with
a day, a week, a month, a year

every with
morning, day, evening, week, year

How often do you . . .

▶ wash your face? *I wash my face three times a day.* _____

1 comb your hair? _____

2 wash your hair? _____

3 brush your teeth? _____

4 have a bath or a shower? _____

5 clean your shoes? _____

6 have a haircut? _____

7 go to the dentist's? _____

8 buy presents for your parents? _____

9 get presents? _____

10 have school holidays? _____

5 Class game

a. Write an action on a strip of paper, like this:

b. Fold the paper so that your action is at the back, like this:

c. Exchange papers with a partner.
Don't read what's on the paper!

d. Now write, for example,
**once a year, twice a week
three times a month, ten times a day**.

e. Read the sentences to the class.

Possible sentences:

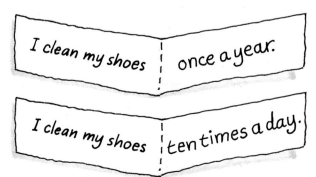

21 Tom plays football

Present simple or continuous? **let's**

Let's talk about Tom.

Tom **loves** football.
He **plays** four times
a week.
He**'s playing** now.
Let's watch.

Let's talk about Nick.

Nick **hates** homework.
But he **does** it
every day.
Look! He**'s doing**
his homework at
the moment.

And I **love** chasing
that stupid cat next door.
I **chase** her every day.
But look! I**'m not chasing**
her just now . . .
not yet . . .

Grammar lesson

Present simple or continuous?

1   We use the present simple for
    repeated actions – things that happen
    (or don't happen) many times or all
    the time.

    We often use it with **always**, **never**,
    once a week, **every day** etc.
    ▶ *We **do** homework **every day**.*
       *Tom usually **plays** football*
       ***four times a week**.*

    We also use it for facts which do not
    change.
    ▶ *Nick **hates** homework.*

2   We use the present continuous for
    something that is happening at the
    moment of speaking.

    We often use it with **now**, **at the
    moment**, **just now**.
    ▶ *Look! Tom's **playing** football **now**.*
       *Nick's **doing** his homework*
       ***at the moment**.*
       *Chip **isn't chasing** Fluff **just now**.*

let's

We use **let's** (or **let us**) for a suggestion.
▶ ***Let's** talk about Tom.*
   ***Let's** watch.*

1 What are they? What are they doing?

Look at the pictures.
Write and say what the people are and what
they are doing. Use the words in the list.

a nurse ✓	boys	a reporter
a doctor	a farmer	pilots
dancers	a policeman	astronauts

4 _____

_____

► *She is a nurse.*
She is eating.

5 _____

_____

1 _____

_____

6 _____

_____

2 _____

_____

7 _____

_____

3 _____

_____

8 _____

_____

2 It's the wrong day

It's Tuesday. Mr and Mrs Bell are doing things today
that they usually do on other days.
Write what they are doing, and when they usually do it.

MR BELL

Wednesdays	plays chess ✓
Thursdays	writes letters
Fridays	plays golf
Saturdays	mows the lawn
Sundays	washes the car

MRS BELL

Mondays	does the shopping
Wednesdays	goes to her art class
Thursdays	does the ironing
Fridays	washes her hair
Saturdays	plays tennis

▶ *He's playing chess today, but he usually plays on Wednesdays.*

1 _____

2 _____

3 _____

4 _____

5 _____

6 _____

7 _____

8 _____

9 _____

3 Zoe and Anna

a You and your partner read about Zoe.
Ask your partner ten questions about Zoe.
Use the present simple and the present
continuous.

> ► YOU   *Is she studying English in Greece?*
>   PARTNER *No, she isn't. She's studying*
>   *English in England.*
>   YOU   *Does she like speaking English?*
>   PARTNER *Yes, she does.*

Zoe

This is Zoe. She is from Greece. She is
thirteen years old. She is studying English
in England. She likes England and she likes
speaking English. She's got a lot of English
books.

She doesn't like music. She plays volleyball.

It is raining today. Zoe and Jenny are
speaking English in the house. Zoe is
making mistakes. They are laughing.

b Now you and your partner read about Anna.
Your partner asks you ten questions
about Anna.

Anna

This is Anna. She is from Greece. She is
thirteen years old. She is visiting England
with her class. She doesn't like England.
She hates speaking English. She hasn't got
any English books.

She plays tennis. She plays the piano.

It isn't raining today. Anna and Amanda are
playing tennis in the park. Anna is losing.
She is making mistakes. She isn't laughing
She isn't having fun.

4 Let's . . .

Make suggestions with **Let's**. Use:

go swimming ✓	read them in bed
put on the light	ask her
hurry	play football
close the window	chase Chip
look for him	have something to drink
watch television	make some sandwiches
go by bus	

> ► It's very hot today. _____
>   *Let's go swimming.*

1 I'm hungry. _____
   _____

2 It's raining. We can't play outside. _____
   _____

3 It's dark in here. _____
   _____

4 It's nice weather today. _____
   _____

5 It's cold in here. _____
   _____

6 I'm thirsty. _____
   _____

7 We're late for school. _____
   _____

8 Trig is hiding. _____
   _____

9 It's a long way. _____
   _____

10 Here's Mum. _____
    _____

11 Chip's chasing the cat. _____
    _____

12 Here are some comics. _____
    _____

22 Was Nick ill?   Past simple of **be** and **have**

NICK	Hello, Mr Blake. I'm phoning about Nick Bell. He **wasn't** at school yesterday. He **was** ill.
MR BLAKE	Oh, dear. **Was** he in bed?
NICK	Yes, he **was**. He **had** a sore throat and a headache.
MR BLAKE	**Did** he **have** a temperature, too?
NICK	No, he **didn't have** a temperature, but he **had** a sore toe, a sore finger and a toothache as well!
MR BLAKE	Oh, **did** he? Who is that speaking, please?
NICK	This is my father.

Grammar lesson

Past simple of **be**

I **was**	I **was not** OR **wasn't**	**was** I?
you **were**	you **were not** OR **weren't**	**were** you?
he **was**	he **was not** OR **wasn't**	**was** he?
she **was**	she **was not** OR **wasn't**	**was** she?
it **was**	it **was not** OR **wasn't**	**was** it?
we **were**	we **were not** OR **weren't**	**were** we?
you **were**	you **were not** OR **weren't**	**were** you?
they **were**	they **were not** OR **weren't**	**were** they?

Also:

there **was**	there **was not** OR **wasn't**	**was** there?
there **were**	there **were not** OR **weren't**	**were** there?

Short answers

Was Nick ill?	**Yes, he was.**
Was he really ill?	**No, he wasn't.**

Past simple of have

I you he she it we you they	**had**	I you he she it we you they **did not** OR **didn't have**

Questions
Did I **have**?
Did he **have**?

Short answers
Did you have a temperature?
Yes, I did. OR **No, I didn't.**
Did your brother have a headache?
Yes, he did. OR **No, he didn't.**

▶ *He **had** a sore throat yesterday.*
***Did** he **have** a temperature, too?*
*No, he **didn't have** a temperature.*

Learn also:
have breakfast, lunch, supper,
a meal, a shower, a bath

1 Where were they yesterday?

Say where they were. Use **was** or **were**.

▶ *Peter was at the theatre.*

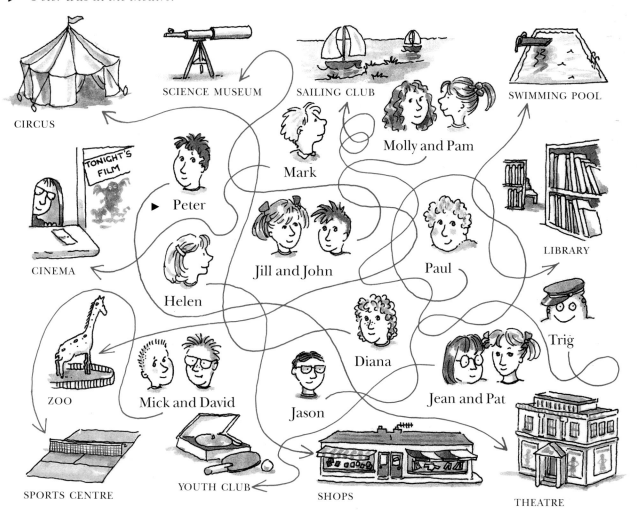

CIRCUS   SCIENCE MUSEUM   SAILING CLUB   SWIMMING POOL

TONIGHT'S FILM

Mark   Molly and Pam

▶ Peter

CINEMA   Helen   Jill and John   Paul   LIBRARY

Diana   Trig

ZOO   Mick and David   Jason   Jean and Pat

SPORTS CENTRE   YOUTH CLUB   SHOPS   THEATRE

2 Famous people quiz

Say who they were. Use **was** or **were**.

▶ *Albert Einstein was a scientist.*
▶ *George Washington and John F. Kennedy were US presidents.*

Homer   Virgil

Beethoven

John F. Kennedy

Columbus

US presidents
composers
scientist
artists
inventor
explorer
writer
poets
film actor
singer
philosophers

Charlie Chaplin

Van Gogh

Picasso

Elvis Presley

Agatha Christie

Mozart

George Washington

Albert Einstein

Marconi

Socrates

Plato

3 Yesterday

Put in **have**, **had** or **didn't have**.

▶ Nick didn't go to school yesterday.
Did he _have_ a temperature?

▶ Yes, poor boy. He _had_ a sore toe
and a sore finger as well.

1 Did Nick _____ a headache and
a sore throat yesterday?

2 Yes, and he _____ a toothache as
well.

3 What time did Nick and Jenny _____
breakfast?

4 Nick wasn't hungry, so he _____
a big breakfast.

5 Jenny _____ a shower. It was too late.

6 Trig was rather late with breakfast, too.
He _____ it at two-thirty.

7 He _____ a shower, because
he hates water.

8 When did Trig _____ lunch
yesterday?

9 He _____ lunch at four o'clock and
he _____ another snack at five o'clock.

10 The family _____ supper at seven
o'clock, as usual.

11 Did Jenny _____ a bath at nine
o'clock?

12 Trig _____ a midnight snack in
bed, as usual.

4 Question time

a Write short answers.

▶ Were you at school yesterday?
Yes, I was. OR _No, I wasn't_.

▶ Did you have a big breakfast this morning?
Yes, I did. OR _No, I didn't_.

1 Were you at home yesterday?
_____

2 Were you ill?
_____

3 Were your friends at school yesterday?
_____

4 Was your father at work yesterday?
_____

5 Were there any letters for you yesterday?
_____

6 Was there a parcel for you?
_____

7 Did you have lunch at home yesterday?
_____

8 Was there a football match on television
yesterday?
_____

9 Was your favourite programme on
television last night?
_____

10 Did you have a bath last night?
_____

11 Did you have cornflakes for breakfast
this morning?
_____

12 Were you late for school this morning?
_____

b Now ask a partner these questions.

23 Did Trig help? Past simple of regular verbs; **ago**

NICK   A few days ago Trig **wanted** to work in the garden. First he **watched** Dad. Then he **filled** the watering-can and **carried** it to the flower-beds. Dad was so pleased. He **stopped** his digging and **smiled**. But he **didn't smile** for long. . . .

TOM   Oh, dear. **Did** Trig 'help' again?

NICK   Oh, yes. He certainly **tried**. He **pulled up** all the flowers and **watered** the weeds!

Grammar lesson

Past simple of regular verbs

Most verbs are regular. Add **ed** or **d** to the base form for the past simple affirmative:

  help → help**ed**   smile → smile**d**

After **did**, **did not** or **didn't**, use only the base form.

▶ *Trig **wanted** to help in the garden.*
   ***Did** he **help**?*
   *Dad **didn't smile** for long.*

I you he she it we you they	} helped	I you he she it we you they	} **did not** OR **didn't help**

Questions
Did I **help**?
Did he **help**?

Short answers
Did you help?   **Yes, I did.**
Did they help?   **No, they didn't.**

We use the past simple for actions that started and finished in the past. We often use them with a time expression.

▶ *A few days **ago** Trig **wanted** to work in the garden. **First** he **watched** Dad.*

Spelling

1 try → tri**ed**   carry → **carried**
   (**y** after a consonant → **ied**.)

2 stop → sto**pped**   plan → pla**nned**
   (One-syllable verbs ending in one vowel + one consonant double the consonant.)

ago

An hour ago means 'an hour before now'. Look where **ago** stands.

▶ *It's six o'clock. Tom arrived an hour **ago**.*
   (= at five o'clock)

Also: a week **ago**, three days **ago**, two years/months **ago**, a few minutes/hours **ago**.

1 Make lists

Write the past simple forms of these verbs. Put them in the correct lists.

love ✓	hate	tidy	fill	bury	plan	study
help ✓	walk	use	arrive	want	dance	clap
stop	pull up	carry	drop	smile	dry	like
try	water	look	hurry	shop	cry	empty

d	**ed**	**ied**	**double consonant + ed**
► *loved*	► *helped*		

---

2 A busy week

Say and write what the Bells did last week.

► mend the fence   MR BELL

Mr Bell mended the fence.

1 oil his bicycle   NICK

2 wash the car   MRS BELL

3 study for a Maths test   JENNY

4 clean the windows   MR BELL

5 tidy the bedrooms   MRS BELL

6 empty all the rubbish bins   NICK

7 bury a smelly bone   CHIP

8 dust the rooms   JENNY

9 paint the bathroom   MRS BELL

10 cook a cheese omelette   JENNY

11 work for a History exam   NICK

12 bake some cakes   MRS BELL

13 help in the garden   TRIG

14 water the weeds   TRIG

3 Famous people

a Who was it? Write in the correct names from the list.

▶ <u>Grace Kelly</u>   lived in America and Monaco. She acted in films.
She married a prince. She died in 1982.

1 _____ lived in England and America. He composed many
famous songs. He died in 1980.

2 _____ lived in England and America.
He acted in funny films. He died in 1977.

3 _____ lived in America. He created Mickey Mouse.
He died in 1966.

4 _____ lived in Italy. He painted the 'Mona Lisa'.
He died in 1519.

5 _____ lived in Russia. She danced in ballets.
She died in 1931.

6 _____ lived in Egypt. She ruled the Egyptians.
She died 2,000 years ago.

Cleopatra   Anna Pavlova
Grace Kelly ✓   Walt Disney
John Lennon   Leonardo da Vinci
Charlie Chaplin

b Now correct these wrong statements.

▶ Walt Disney lived in England.
He didn't live in England. He lived in America.

▶ Anna Pavlova acted in films.
She didn't act in films. She danced in ballets.

1 Cleopatra lived in France.

_____

2 John Lennon died in 1970.

_____

3 Walt Disney created Asterix.

_____

4   Anna Pavlova lived in Spain.

_____

5   Grace Kelly danced in ballets.

_____

6   Anna Pavlova died in 1920.

_____

7   Charlie Chaplin painted the 'Mona Lisa'.

_____

8   Cleopatra died in 1975.

_____

9   Charlie Chaplin lived in Russia.

_____

10   John Lennon directed films.

_____

11   Leonardo da Vinci created Mickey Mouse.

_____

12   Walt Disney composed songs.

_____

4 Did she? Did he?

With a partner, ask or answer ten questions about the famous people in Exercise 3. Give short answers.

▶ Did Grace Kelly live in Monaco?
Yes, she did.
▶ Did Walt Disney die in 1519?
No, he didn't.

5 What about you?

Answer the questions with **ago**.

▶ When was your birthday?
About three months ago. OR *Two weeks ago.*

1 When was your best friend's birthday?
2 When did you learn to swim?
3 When did you get your first bicycle?
4 When did you start school?
5 When was your last visit to the zoo?
6 When did you get your last pocket money?
7 When was the last school holiday?
8 When was your last English test?
9 When did you last go to the dentist's?
10 When did you get your watch?

24 Nick lost his money   Past simple of irregular verbs

Nick can't find his money.

JENNY   Well, where **did** you **go** yesterday?

NICK   I **went** to the sports shop on the bus. I **bought** some new wheels for my skateboard.

JENNY   Perhaps you **left** your money in the bus.

NICK   No, I **didn't**. I **paid** for the wheels.

JENNY   Perhaps you **lost** it in the shop.

NICK   No, I **didn't lose** it in the shop.

JENNY   **Did** you **spend** it all on a present for me . . . ?

Grammar lesson

Past simple of irregular verbs

In the past simple, irregular verbs have special affirmative forms. You must learn these forms. There is a list at the back of this book.

We make the negative and the question forms with **did not** or **didn't** and **did** . . . + base form, as for regular verbs.

| I you he she it we you they | **went** | I you he she it we you they | **did not** OR **didn't go** |

Questions
Did I **go**?
Did he **go**?

Short answers
Did you go?   **Yes, I did.**
Did he go?   **No, he didn't.**

1 Pairs

Find and write ten pairs.

Base form	Past simple
▶ lose	▶ lost

lose ✓	found	paid	come
sing	give	gave	build
came	bought	pay	find
spent	buy	left	go
sang	ran	spend	went
run	leave	built	lost ✓

2 More pairs

Find and say pairs.

▶ *make, made*
▶ *get, got*

	Base form	Past simple			Base form	Past simple
a	make	fell		b	dig	did
	get	brought			drink	stood
	fly	broke			think	was
	break	sat			do	told
	fall	swam			tell	had
	bring	got			stand	began
	write	wrote			be	thought
	take	took			have	knew
	sit	flew			know	dug
	swim	made			begin	drank
	see	ate				
	eat	saw				

3 A summer holiday

Put in the past simple forms.
Use all the verbs from Exercise 2a, like this:

Last year the Bells ▶ *flew* _____ to
Greece on holiday. They ¹_____
the Parthenon and many other buildings and
they ²_____ a lot of Greek food.

They ³_____ on the beach in
the sun and ⁴_____ in the warm sea.
Nick and Jenny ⁵_____ some
Greek friends. They ⁶_____ a lot of
postcards to their friends in England and
they ⁷_____ a lot of photographs.
They all ⁸_____ sunburned.

Unfortunately Mr Bell ⁹_____
down the hotel steps and ¹⁰_____
his arm! But he ¹¹_____ home
many other souvenirs as well.

4 Trig can do it. Can you?

Try to write correct sentences.

► | did | Where | go | last year | the Bells | ?   ► | see | they | Did | the Parthenon | ?

| Where | did | the Bells | go | last year | ?

__Where did the Bells go last year?__

| Did | they | see | the Parthenon | ?

__Did they see the Parthenon?__

1 | they | sit | Did | on the beach | ?

_____

2 | What | they | eat | did | ?

_____

3 | do | What | did | on the beach | Nick and Jenny | ?

_____

4 | they | Did | get | sunburned | ?

_____

5 | postcards | many | Did | write | they | ?

_____

6 | Did | take | photographs | they | ?

_____

7 | Where | they | swim | did | ?

_____

8 | did | What | Mr Bell | break | ?

_____

9 | fall | Where | he | did | ?

_____

10 | Did | bring | home | he | other souvenirs | ?

_____

5 Your holidays

a   Answer the questions with full sentences.

▶   Did you go on holiday last year? *Yes, I went on holiday last year.*

_____

▶   How many presents or souvenirs did you buy? *I bought two presents for my best friends, Jane and Sarah.*

1   When did you last go on holiday? _____

_____

2   How did you travel? By car or by train? _____

_____

3   Did you fly? _____

_____

4   Where did you go? _____

_____

5   Where did you stay? In a hotel or with friends? _____

_____

6   Did you go with your parents? _____

_____

7   What did you do during the day? _____

_____

8   What did you do in the evenings? _____

_____

9   What did you see? _____

_____

10   Did you write postcards to your friends at home? _____

_____

11   How much money did you spend? _____

_____

12   Did you make new friends? _____

_____

13   What did you eat? _____

_____

14   Did you fall and break an arm or a leg? _____

_____

b   Now give a short answer where suitable.

25 What's Trig going to do? be going to

JENNY   Look, there's Trig. What**'s** he **going to do**?

NICK   He's got the lawn mower. He**'s going to mow** the lawn. And look at those clouds! It**'s going to rain**.

JENNY   Look. He **isn't going to mow** the lawn. He's pushing the lawn mower into the house.

NICK   Oh no! **Is** he **going to mow** the carpets?

Grammar lesson

be going to

1   Use **be going to** + base form for a future intention or plan.

I **am**
you **are**
he **is**
she **is**   } **going to mow** the lawn.
it **is**
we **are**
you **are**
they **are**

▶ *I am not* OR *I'm not going to mow the lawn.*
Are you going to mow the lawn?

Short answers
Is he going to mow the carpet?
Yes, he is. OR **No, he isn't.**

2   Use **be going to** for a prediction, when something in the present tells us about the future.
▶ *Look at those black clouds!*
It's going to rain.

1   What are they going to do?

Match sentences from the two columns.
Then write new sentences with **be going to**.

▶   Mr Bell is hot.   go to bed early
1   Chip's thirsty.   watch television
2   Jenny's tired.   have a drink
3   Mrs Bell's ill.   ask his mother
4   Nick's bored.   look for him in the garden
5   Chip and Trig are hungry.   have a cold shower
6   Mr Todd's cold.   put on the light
7   Amanda and Mrs Todd are wet.   turn down the radio
8   Tom can't do his homework.   miss the next football match
9   It's dark. Tom can't see.   get some food from the fridge
10 It's loud. Mrs Todd can't hear.   have a hot bath
11 Tom's got a broken leg.   see his dentist
12 Jenny can't find Chip.   dry their clothes
13 Mr Bell can't start the car.   take some tablets
14 Nick's got a toothache.   telephone the garage

▶   *He's going to have a cold shower.*

1   _____

2   _____

3   _____

4   _____

5   _____

6   _____

7   _____

8   _____

9   _____

10 _____

11 _____

12 _____

13 _____

14 _____

2 At the weekend

Say what you **are going to** do, or **are not going to** do,
at the weekend.

▶ visit a friend
   I'm going to visit a friend.
▶ wash my hair
   I'm not going to wash my hair.

tidy your room?	visit an aunt or uncle?	sit in the sun?
sleep late?	drive to the sea?	play football?
watch television?	help in the house?	write letters?
phone your friends?	play computer games?	go shopping?

3 Future plans

These pupils already have plans for their future jobs.
Match what they like or can do with what they are going to do.
Then write new sentences with **be going to**.

▶	Barbara likes animals.	become a pilot
1	Mark is good at Maths.	become a kindergarten teacher
2	Pam likes cooking.	work in a bank
3	Sam loves aeroplanes.	become a vet
4	Jane loves small children.	become a train driver
5	Scott loves trains.	study art
6	Sarah is good at painting.	study medicine
7	Pat wants to be a doctor.	buy a restaurant
8	Ann loves computers.	become an author
9	Paul likes writing stories.	become a sports teacher
10	Bill loves sports.	study computer science

▶ *Barbara's going to become a vet.*
1 _____
2 _____
3 _____
4 _____
5 _____
6 _____
7 _____
8 _____
9 _____
10 _____

4 What's going to happen?

Look at the picture. Write what**'s going to** happen or what
the people **are going to** do.

▶ _She's going to answer the phone._

6 _____

1 _____

7 _____

2 _____

8 _____

3 _____

9 _____

4 _____

10 _____

5 _____

Oxford University Press
Walton Street, Oxford OX2 6DP

Oxford New York Toronto Madrid
Delhi Bombay Calcutta Madras Karachi
Kuala Lumpur Singapore Hong Kong Tokyo
Nairobi Dar es Salaam Cape Town
Melbourne Auckland

and associated companies in
Berlin Ibadan

OXFORD and OXFORD ENGLISH
are trade marks of Oxford University Press.

ISBN 0 19 431361 1
ISBN 0 19 431354 9 (Greek edition)
© Oxford University Press 1992

First published 1992
Fourth impression 1993

Illustrated by Heather Clarke
Typeset by Pentacor PLC

Printed in Hong Kong